Straight Lines

■ Draw a line from one picture to the matching picture.

Name

Date

P9-DDS-255

To parents
Write your child's name and the date in the boxes. Do the exercise along with your child if he or she has difficulty. If your child is not familiar with drawing lines, practice scribbling on scrap paper first.

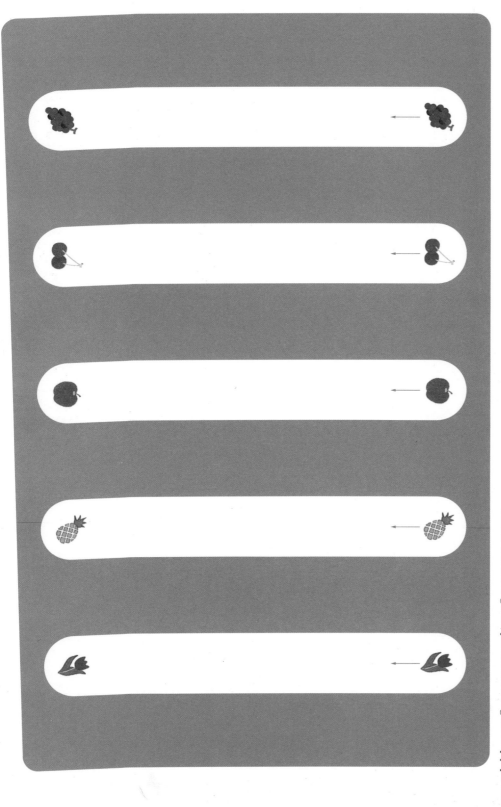

1

■ Draw a line from one picture to the matching picture.

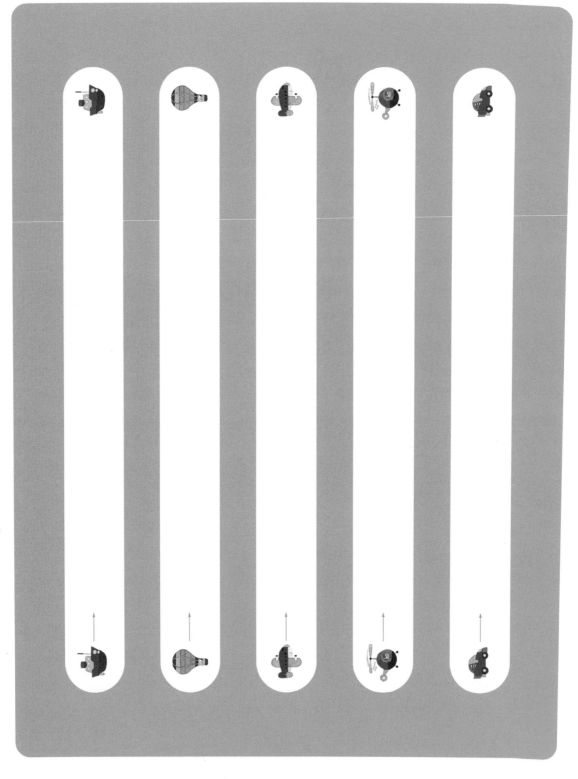

Curved Lines

■ Draw a line from one picture to the matching picture.

Name

Date

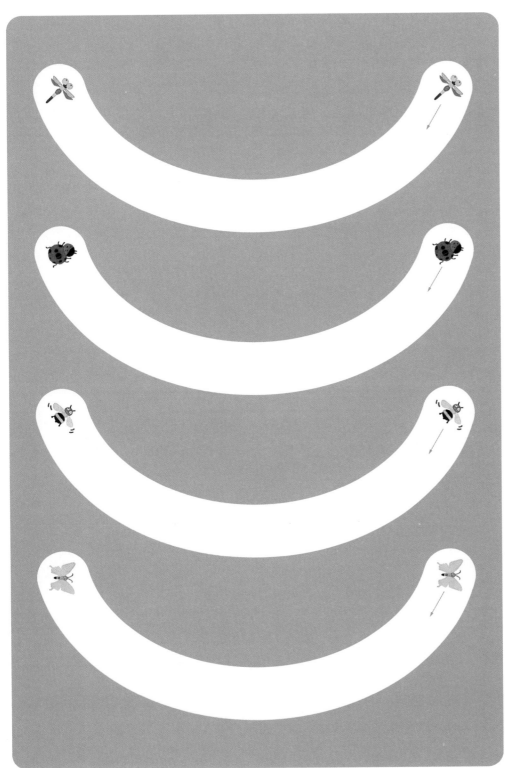

■ Draw a line from one picture to the matching picture.

4

Diagonal Lines

Draw a line from one picture to the matching picture.

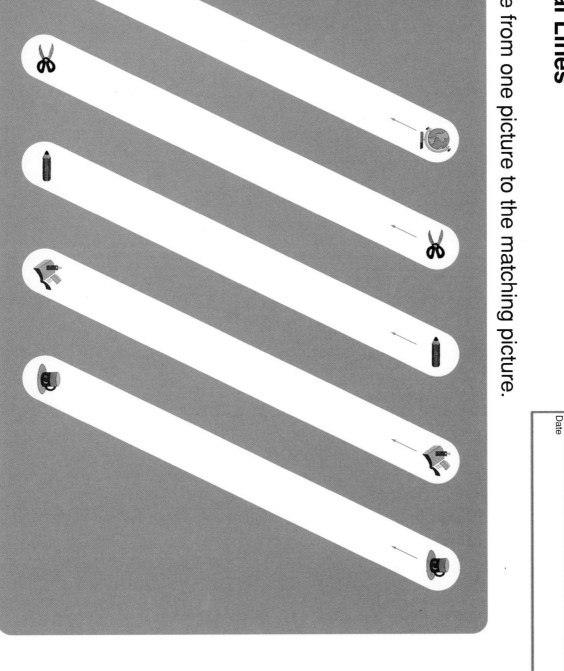

■ Draw a line from one picture to the matching picture.

6

Wavy Lines

■ Draw a line from one picture to the matching picture.

Name

Date

7

■ Draw a line from one picture to the matching picture.

Connect the Numbers

■ Draw a line from 1 to 10 in order while saying each number.

Name

Date

To parents
It is okay if your child draws outside the path. Encourage your child to move the pencil slowly along the curved path.

Balloons

■ Draw a line from 1 to 10 in order while saying each number.

Top

Connect the Numbers

■ Draw a line from 1 to 15 in order while saying each number.

Name

Date

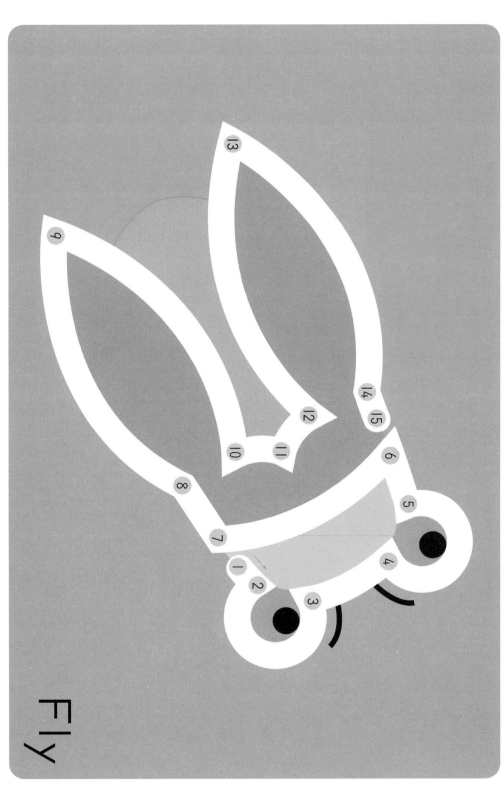

Fly

■ Draw a line from 1 to 15 in order while saying each number.

Butterfly

Connect the Numbers

Draw a line from 1 to 20 in order while saying each number.

Name

Date

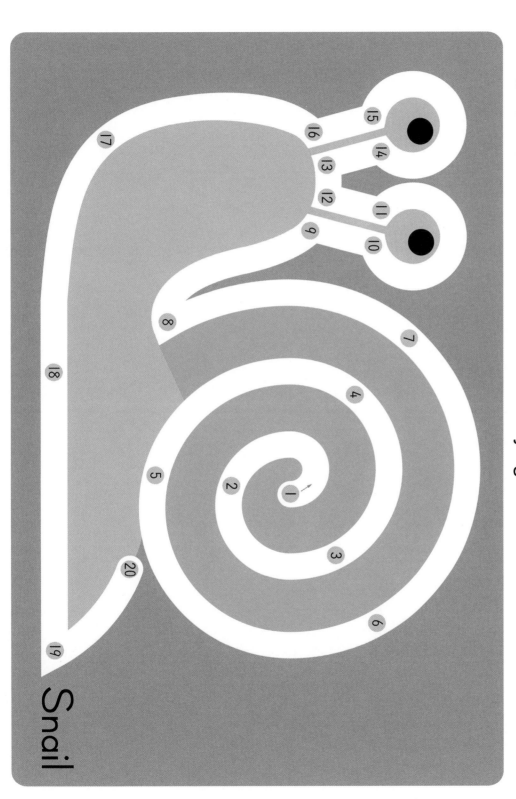

Snail

■ Draw a line from 1 to 20 in order while saying each number.

Dragonfly

Connect the Numbers

■ Draw a line from 1 to 25 in order while saying each number.

Name

Date

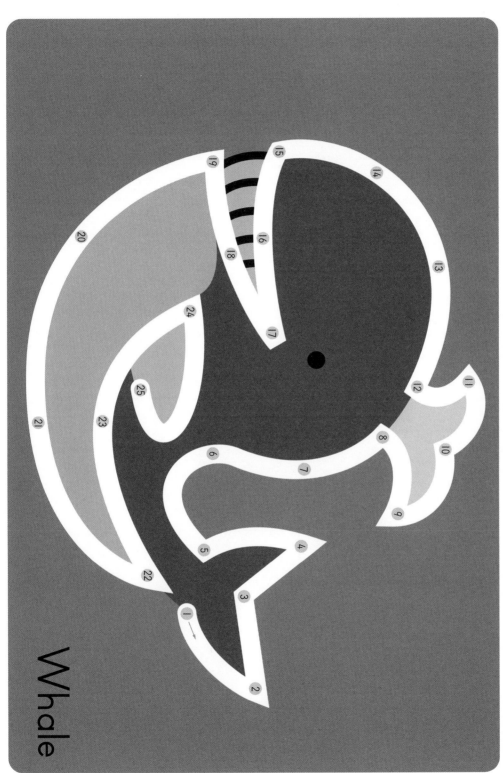

Whale

■ Draw a line from 1 to 25 in order while saying each number.

Horse

Connect the Numbers

Draw a line from 1 to 30 in order while saying each number.

Grapes

■ Draw a line from 1 to 30 in order while saying each number.

Stump

Connect the Numbers

■ Draw a line from 1 to 10 in order while saying each number.

To parents
If it is difficult for your child to draw a line from 1 to 10 with a single stroke, allow him or her to pause at each number.

Bird

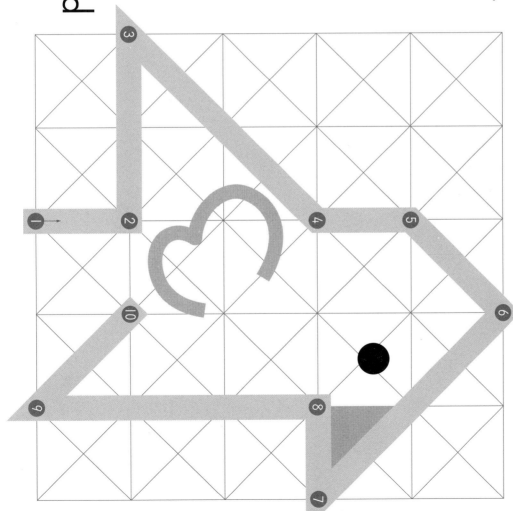

■ Draw a line from 1 to 10 in order while saying each number.

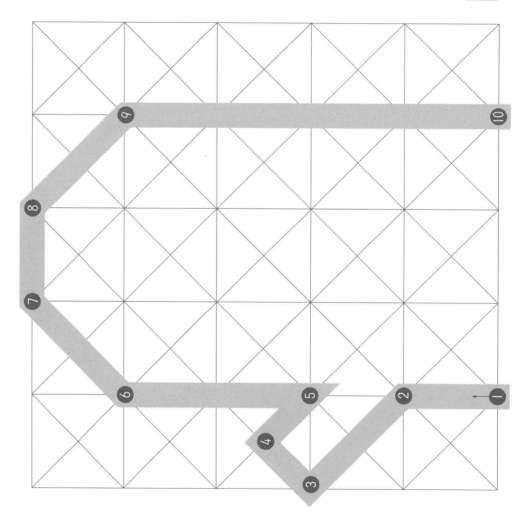

Mitten

Connect the Numbers

- Draw a line from 1 to 12 in order while saying each number.

Spaceship

■ Draw a line from 11 to 20 in order while saying each number.

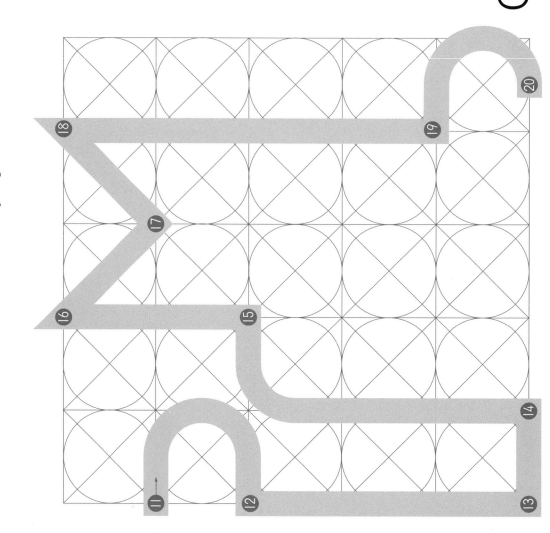

Cat

Connect the Numbers

■ Draw a line from 15 to 25 in order while saying each number.

Name

Date

Koala

■ Draw a line from 12 to 25 in order while saying each number.

Dragonfly

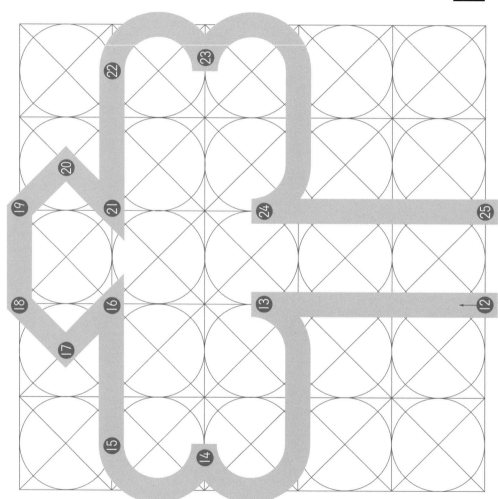

Connect the Numbers

13

■ Draw a line from 21 to 30 in order
while saying each number.

Name

Date

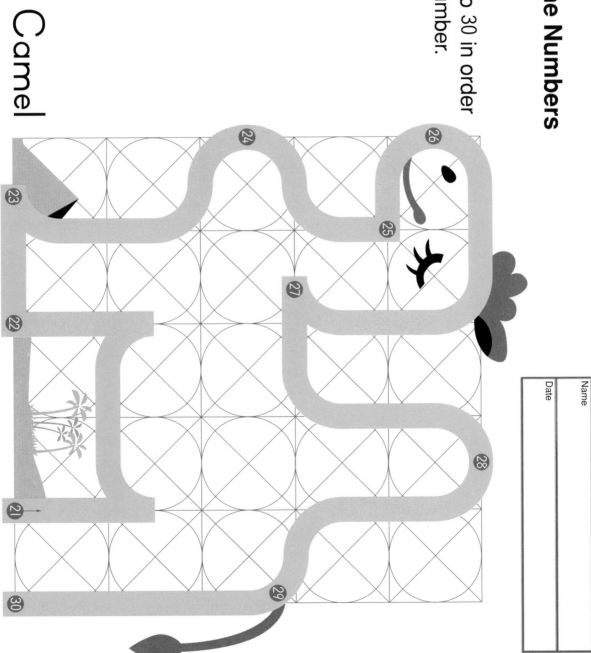

Camel

■ Draw a line from 15 to 30 in order while saying each number.

Elephant

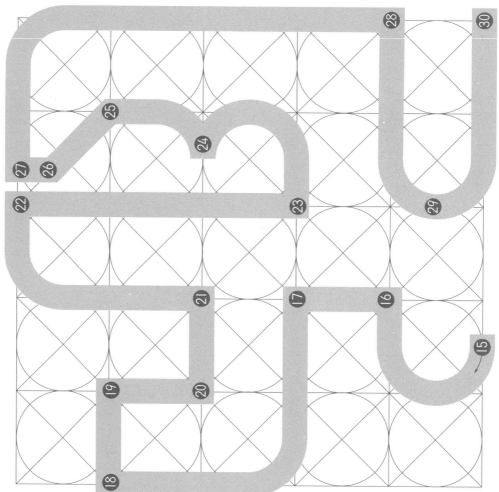

Connect the Numbers

Draw a line from 1 to 10 in order while saying each number.

Name

Date

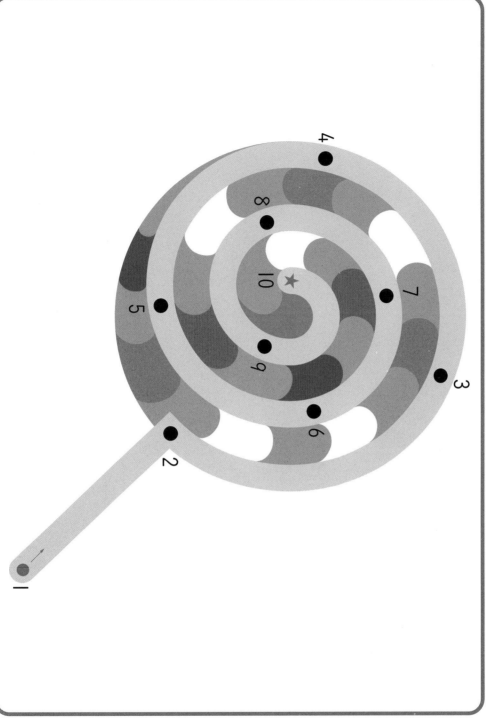

Lollipop

■ Draw a line from 1 to 10 in order while saying each number.

Connect the Numbers

Name

Date

■ Draw a line from 1 to 15 in order while saying each number.

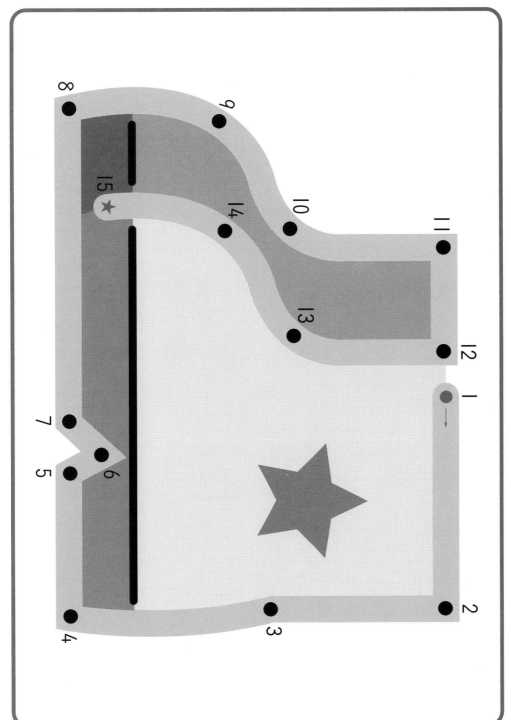

Boots

■ Draw a line from 1 to 15 in order while saying each number.

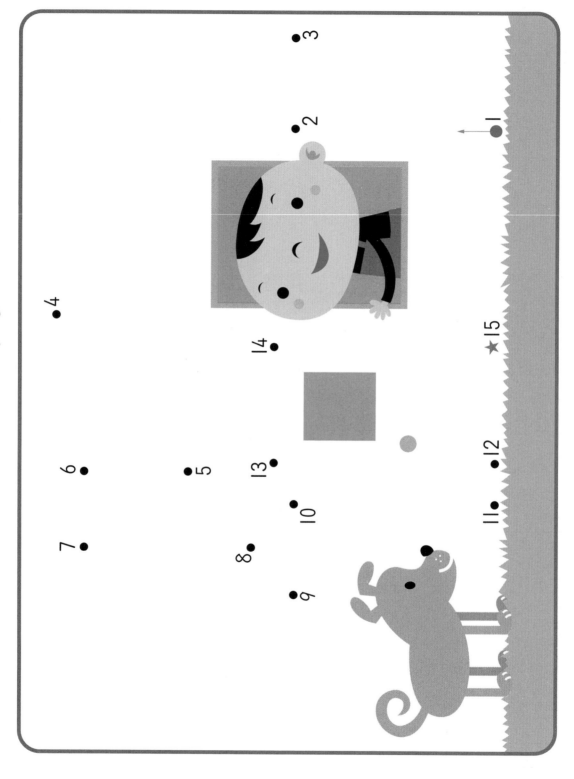

Connect the Numbers

■ Draw a line from 1 to 20 in order while saying each number.

Name

Date

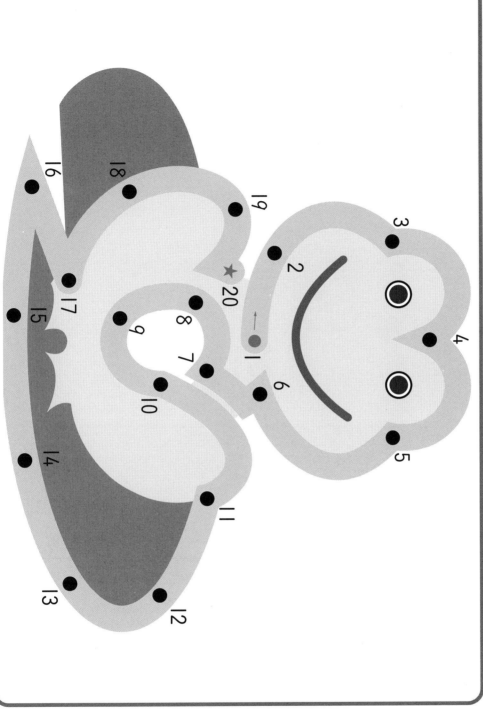

Frog

■ Draw a line from 1 to 20 in order while saying each number.

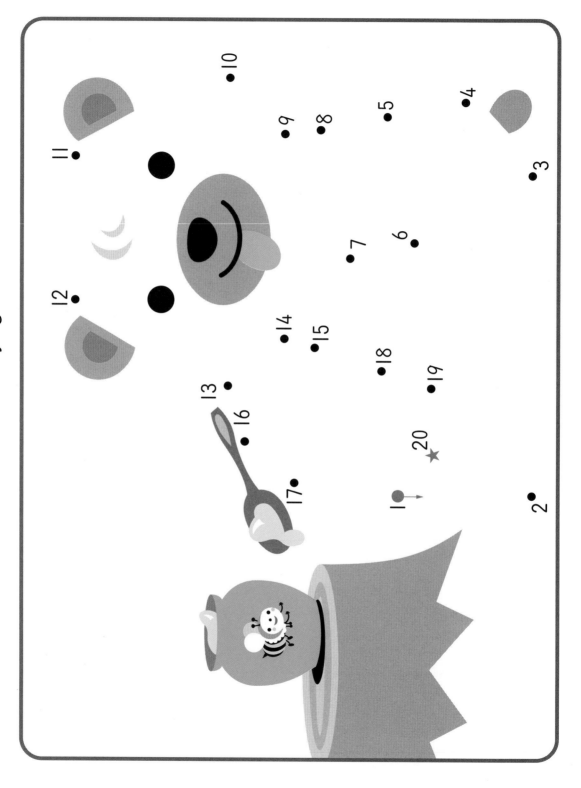

Connect the Numbers

Draw a line from 1 to 30 in order while saying each number.

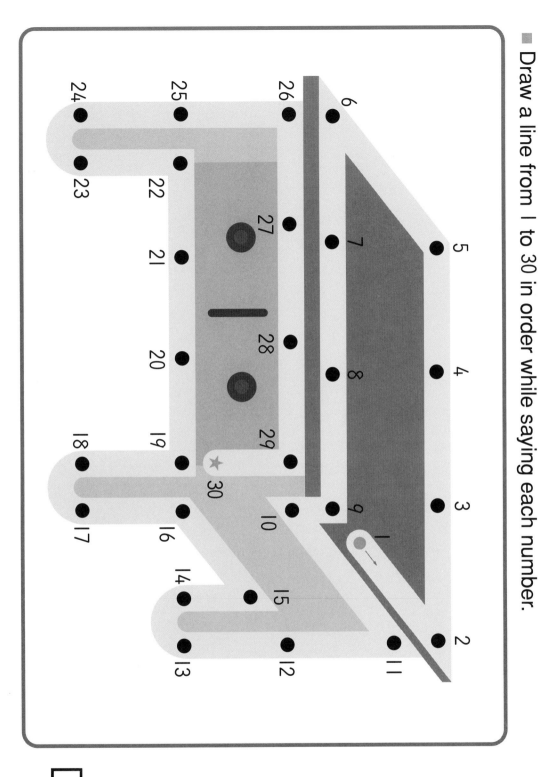

Desk

Name

Date

■ Draw a line from 1 to 30 in order while saying each number.

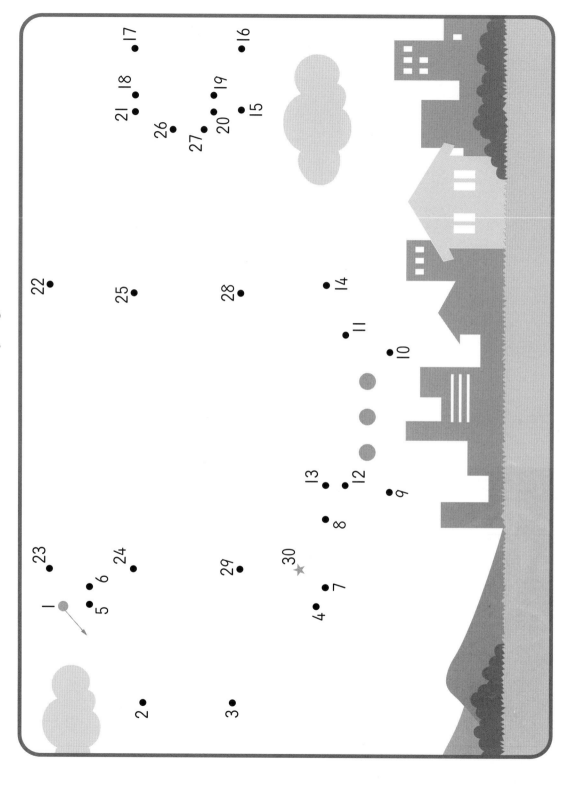

Connect the Numbers

■ Draw a line from 1 to 30 in order while saying each number.

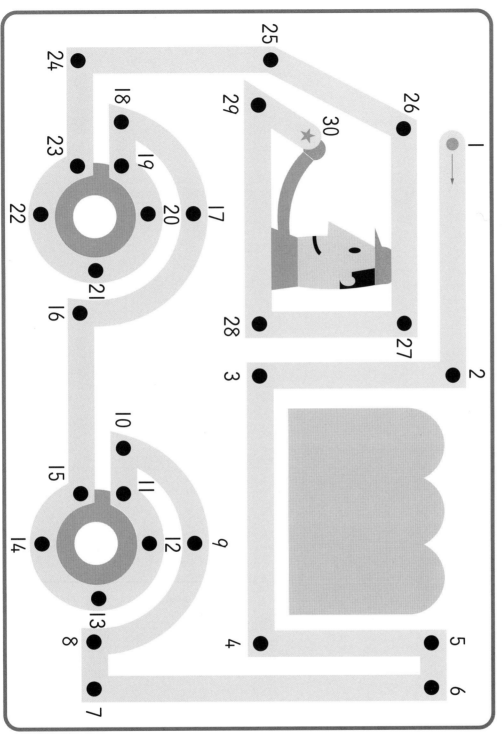

Name

Date

Truck

35

■ Draw a line from 1 to 30 in order while saying each number.

Writing Numbers 1 and 2

■ Write the number 1 and say it aloud.

Name

Date

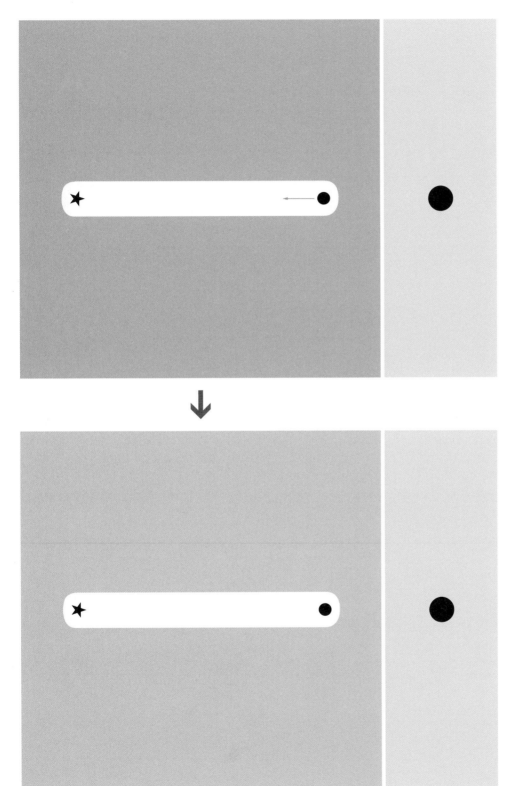

■ Write the number 2 and say it aloud.

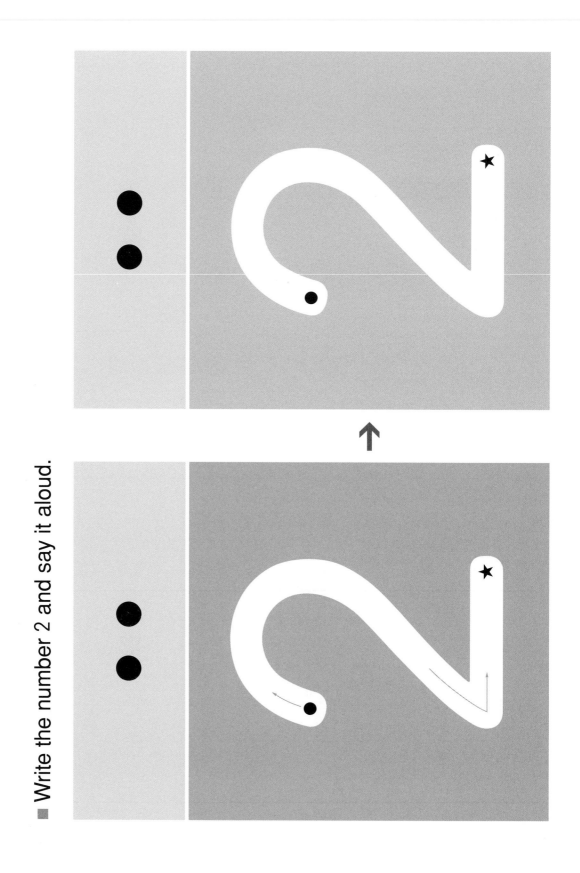

Writing Numbers 3 and 4

Write the number 3 and say it aloud.

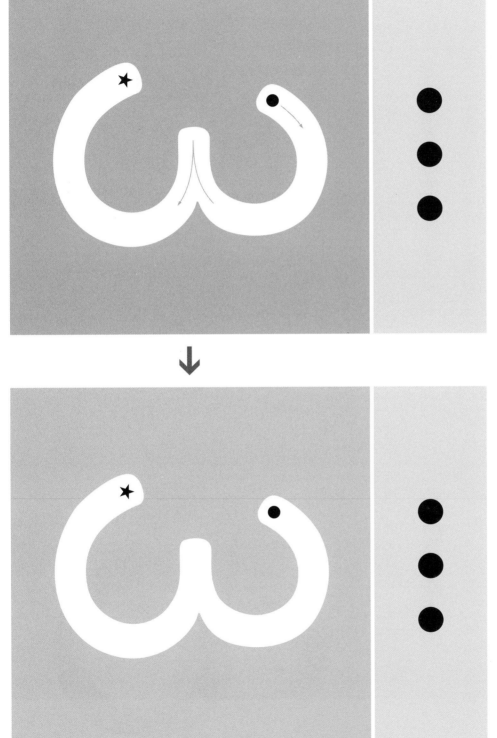

Name

Date

■ Write the number 4 and say it aloud.

To parents
First, demonstrate how to write the number 4 with two strokes. Guide your child's hand if necessary, then have him or her start writing from ① again.

Writing Numbers 5 and 6

Write the number 5 and say it aloud.

Name

Date

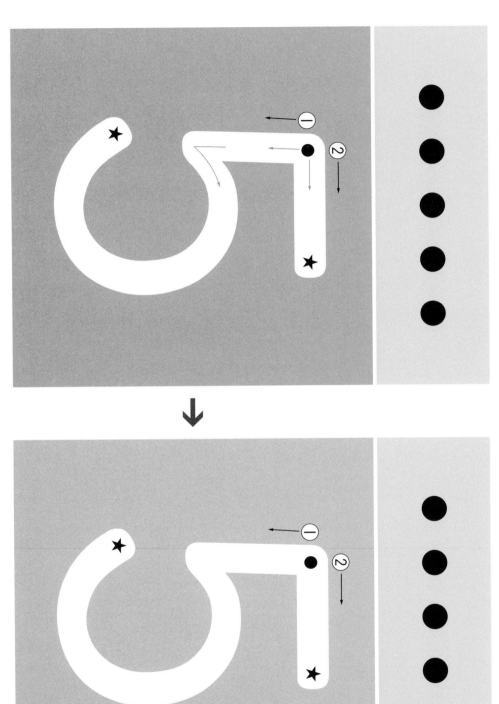

■ Write the number 6 and say it aloud.

Writing Numbers 7 and 8

■ Write the number 7 and say it aloud.

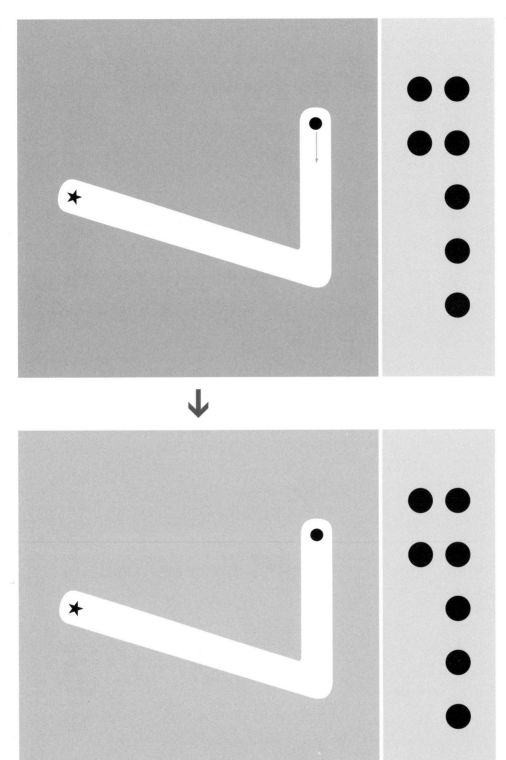

Name _____

Date _____

■ Write the number 8 and say it aloud.

23 Writing Numbers 9 and 10

■ Write the number 9 and say it aloud.

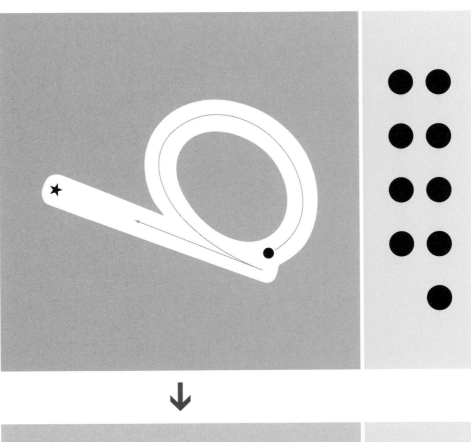

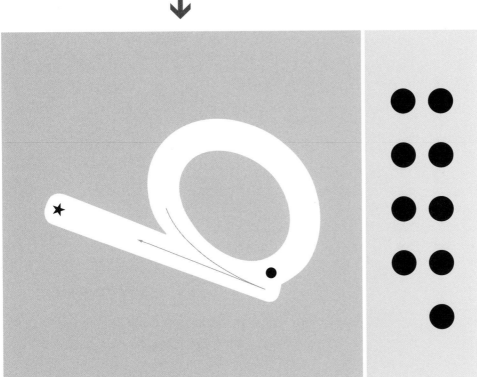

Name

Date

■ Write the number 10 and say it aloud.

Writing Numbers 1 to 4

Write the numbers and say them aloud.

Name	
Date	

■ Write the numbers and say them aloud.

25 Writing Numbers 5 to 8

■ Write the numbers and say them aloud.

■ Write the numbers and say them aloud.

Writing Numbers 9 to 12

■ Write the numbers and say them aloud.

Name

Date

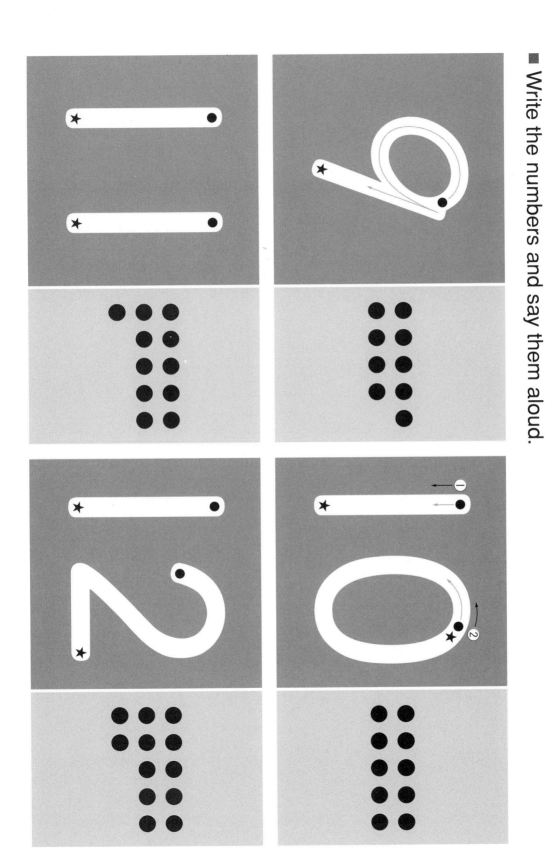

■ Write the numbers and say them aloud.

27 Writing Numbers 13 to 16

■ Write the numbers and say them aloud.

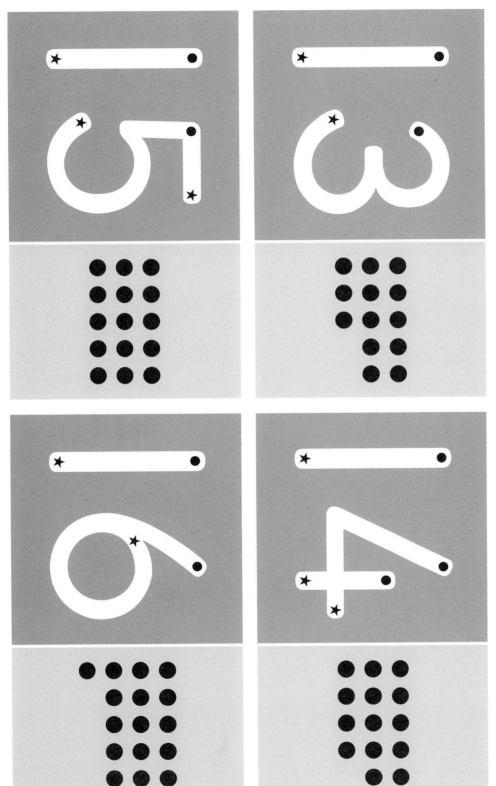

Name	
Date	

■ Write the numbers and say them aloud.

28 Writing Numbers 17 to 20

■ Write the numbers and say them aloud.

■ Write the numbers and say them aloud.

Writing Numbers 1 to 8

■ Write the numbers and say them aloud.

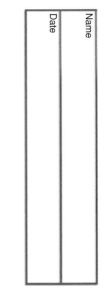

Name

Date

3 ● ★

● ● ●

1 ★ ●

●

2 ● ★

● ●

4 ① ● ★ ● ② ★

● ● ● ●

57

■ Write the numbers and say them aloud.

Writing Numbers 9 to 16

■ Write the numbers and say them aloud.

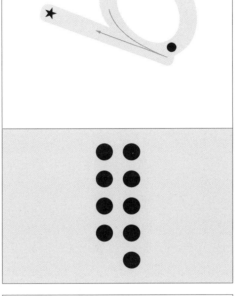

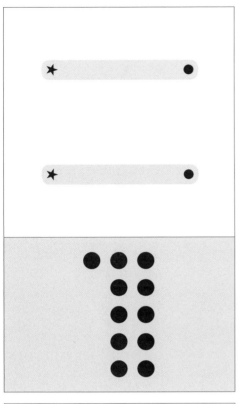

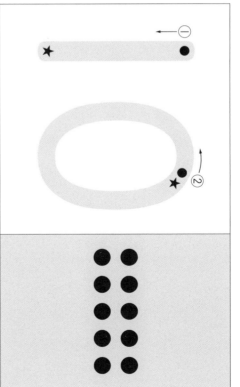

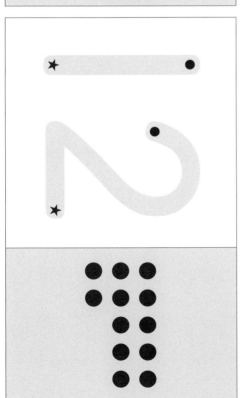

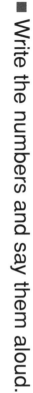

Name	
Date	

59

■ Write the numbers and say them aloud.

Writing Numbers 17 to 24

■ Write the numbers and say them aloud.

Name

Date

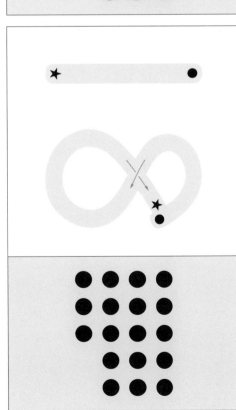

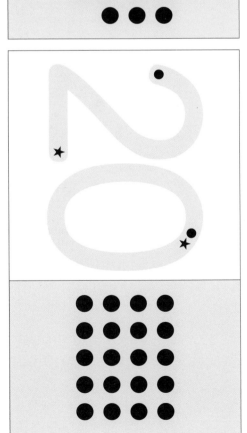

■ Write the numbers and say them aloud.

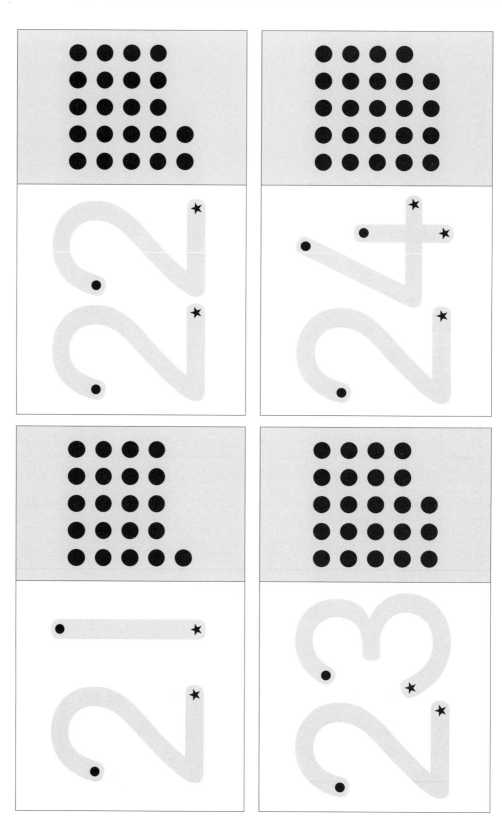

Writing Numbers 25 to 30

■ Write the numbers and say them aloud.

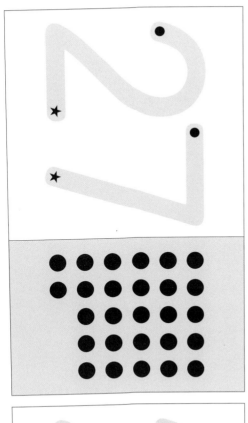

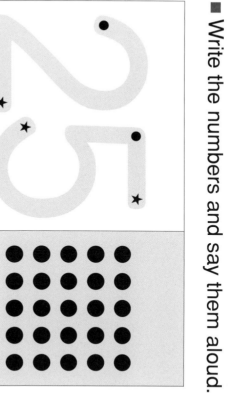

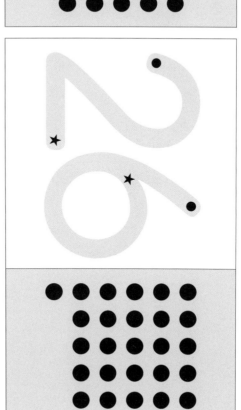

■ Write the numbers and say them aloud.

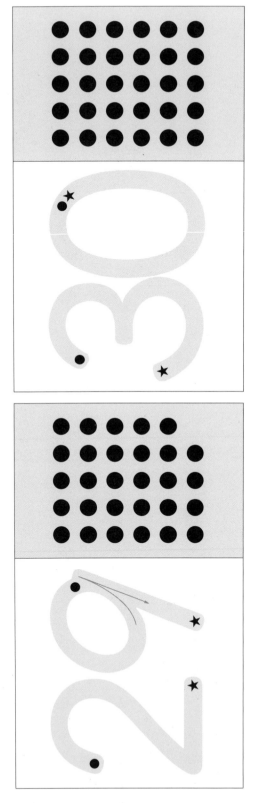